CONCISE COLLECTION

Dinosaurs

Rupert Matthews

Grange
BOOKS

Published in 1995
by Grange Books
An imprint of Grange Books Plc.
The Grange
Grange Yard
London SE1 3AG

ISBN 1 85627 767 4

Printed in Italy.

Acknowledgments
All artworks supplied by Maltings Partnership

Right: Pachycephalosaurus was much larger at 4.5m (15ft) than any other
bone-headed dinosaur of which it was the last, becoming extinct 65
million years ago. It was a plant-eater equipped with sharp teeth which
would have been used to shred, rather than grind, its food. Its skull was
entirely unlike any other and justifies its name, which means 'thick-
headed lizard'. The small brain was encased in a massive skull, the roof of
which consisted of 25cm (10in) of solid bone.

It is now thought that *Pachycephalosaurus* may have engaged in
head-butting fights with each other. The rival dinosaurs would come
together with a terrific clash, but the thick skull would have saved the
brain from injury while the spine absorbed the shock of impact. After
several such collisions, the weaker animal would retire.

Contents

What is a Dinosaur?

The dinosaurs were a large and extremely successful group of prehistoric reptiles which dominated life on land for 150 million years, and spread to every continent on Earth. They were the most important form of life on Earth for nearly three times as long as the mammals have occupied the same position. Compared to the rule of the dinosaurs, our 3 million year history seems paltry. Clearly the dinosaurs were highly successful and superbly adapted to their role, but what exactly is a dinosaur?

The most important feature of the dinosaurs is their amazing variety. There is no such thing as a 'typical dinosaur'. In size dinosaurs ranged from a creature no larger than a chicken to a giant capable of peering over a 6-storey office block. Some dinosaurs plodded slowly on four, pillar-like legs – others raced on two legs at speeds approaching that of a galloping horse. Many species of dinosaur munched contentedly on leaves and fruits, while others tore animals apart with ferocious claws and teeth.

Given this diversity it might appear that scientists would have difficulty placing the dinosaurs within a single group. In fact all dinosaurs share certain characteristics which set them apart from other reptiles. First, dinosaurs have an erect posture so that their legs are tucked underneath the body, like those of a mammal, and do not splay outwards as do the limbs of a lizard. Secondly their teeth are set in individual sockets in the jaw, while other reptiles have their teeth let into a long groove which runs the length of the jaw. Finally dinosaurs have three large holes, or windows, set into the skull. These openings serve to lighten the skull without weakening its structure. Most reptiles have one or two such windows but not three.

These characteristics are shared by all dinosaurs, but some scientists do not think that they constitute a single group. They prefer to divide the dinosaurs into two groups, the ornithischian, or bird-hipped, and saurischian, or reptile-hipped. The division is based upon the shape of the hip bones.

The dinosaurs lived in a world very different from our own. Not only were the dinosaurs unlike modern wildlife, but the vegetation and smaller fauna were also very different. For most of the Age of Dinosaurs, the plant life was dominated by non-flowering species. Ground cover consisted chiefly of ferns and horsetails while conifer forests covered large areas. Plants now extinct, such as palm-like cycads, were common and formed the main food for plant-eating dinosaurs. Towards the end of the Age of Dinosaurs more modern plants appeared. These included trees such as oaks and elms, flowering shrubs and small annuals.

Mammals first evolved during the time of the dinosaurs, but they remained small and unimportant. It is possible that mammals were nocturnal animals or that they lived in dense undergrowth where they could find food unavailable to the larger dinosaurs. Soon after the appearance of the first dinosaurs, a new group of reptiles evolved as flying animals. These pterosaurs survived until 65 million years ago and dominated the skies. They had leathery wings and furry bodies, rather like bats, but were reptilian in origin. The largest pterosaurs were as big as a modern light aircraft, while the smallest were the size of a sparrow. Birds did not evolve until around 150 million years ago, but did not become common until much later.

Dinosaur Families

The Age of Dinosaurs, or the Mesozoic Era, began 225 million years ago and ended 65 million years ago. Geologists have divided it into three periods: the Triassic, Jurassic and Cretaceous. Dinosaurs lived in each of these periods, but the types of dinosaur changed greatly with time. Scientists have categorized the many types of dinosaur into a number of families, which are in turn gathered together in larger groupings. The exact relationships between these various families is still unclear due to gaps in the fossil record. However, it is possible to sketch out the main directions of dinosaur evolution, and the types of dinosaur produced.

There are two basic groups of dinosaur, those with reptile-shaped hips, the saurischian, and those with bird-shaped hips, the ornithischian. Saurischian dinosaurs appeared first, in the mid-Triassic period. These were small, lightly built meat-eaters such as *Coelophysis* (page 14). By the early Jurassic period (about 190 million years ago) larger more heavily built hunters had appeared. Both these groups of dinosaurs survived until the end of the Mesozoic. During the Cretaceous other types of meat-eating saurischian evolved. These included the massive *Tyrannosaurus* (page 44) and the fast-moving *Deinonychus* (page 16) together with the curious toothless ostrich dinosaurs such as *Struthiomimus* (page 40).

Meanwhile a second group of saurischian dinosaurs had taken to eating plants. These sauropods were very successful during the Jurassic period (195–135 million years ago). The basic body pattern of the sauropods remained constant. They had heavy, massive bodies supported on four pillar-like legs. Long tails and necks were carried by all sauropods, which included some of the longest and heaviest animals ever to have lived.

The saurischian sauropods became increasingly uncommon during the Cretaceous period (135–65 million years ago) as the ornithischians took over the role of plant-eating dinosaur. The first ornithischians were small, two-legged herbivores which lived about 200 million years ago. The ornithischians remained unimportant for about 50 million years, when they began evolving into a wide variety of different families. In the Jurassic two groups became quadrupeds. These were the stegosaurs, such as *Stegosaurus* (page 39) and the armoured dinosaurs such as *Hylaeosaurus* (page 22).

Meanwhile large bipedal forms, such as *Iguanodon* (page 23), were becoming common, later evolving into hadrosaurs such as *Parasaurolophus* (page 31) and the bone-head *Pachycephalosaurus* (page 4). A final group of ornithischian dinosaurs did not appear until the close of the Mesozoic. The horned dinosaurs included beasts such as *Triceratops* (page 43) and were highly successful for a short period.

Albertosaurus

Albertosaurus was one of the largest meat-eating dinosaurs of all. It measured about 9m (30ft) in length, weighed nearly 2 tons and walked on its hind legs. This dinosaur was equipped with a fearsome array of teeth with which it may have attacked and killed other dinosaurs. The body of *Albertosaurus* was lightly built for its size, so the creature was probably fairly agile and active. It may have hunted hadrosaurid dinosaurs, such as *Edmontosaurus* (page 19) and *Parasaurolophus* (page 31), which lived at the same time. *Albertosaurus* lived in North America about 65 million years ago, during the Upper Cretaceous period.

The first fossil of *Albertosaurus* to be found was a jawbone filled with extremely sharp teeth. The jaw was discovered about 100 years ago in Alberta, Canada, a fact which gave the dinosaur its name. Over the following years many other fossils were found which came from large meat-eating dinosaurs. At the time scientists thought that these were from different types of animal and gave them different names. Only when a nearly complete *Albertosaurus* skeleton was discovered was it realized that all the bones came from the one type of animal. Since then, many other fossilized remains of *Albertosaurus* have been found. One of these was a young animal. It was much slimmer than an adult, and had proportionally longer jaws and larger eyes – similar features are found in the young of modern reptiles.

Anchisaurus

Fossils of *Anchisaurus* were among the very first dinosaur remains to be found in North America. The first bones were excavated in the Connecticut Valley in 1818, but nobody knew what they were. Not until much later did scientists realize that the bones belonged to a dinosaur. Since then the fossils of many similar dinosaurs have been found. These have been given several different names, such as *Nyasasaurus* and *Thecodontosaurus* (page 42), but scientists have decided that they all belong to the Anchisaurid family of dinosaurs.

Anchisaurus itself measured about 2m (6½ft) in length and usually walked on all fours. The 'thumbs' of its front feet bore large claws which may have been used in feeding. The food which *Anchisaurus* ate has been the subject of much debate. The creature belonged to a group of dinosaurs known as prosauropods, most of whom were herbivores, but the teeth of *Anchisaurus* were fairly sharp and serrated. It has been suggested that *Anchisaurus* ate both meat and plants and could have been an early dinosaur in the process of evolving from flesh-eating ancestors into plant-eating descendants.

Anchisaurus fossils have been found in South Africa as well as North America, indicating that the two continents were joined together around 200 million years ago when this creature lived.

Apatosaurus

Apatosaurus is one of the best known of all dinosaurs, though it is better known under the name of *Brontosaurus*. The confusion of names is due to the way in which the fossils were discovered.

In 1879 two fossil collectors working for the great fossil hunter Othniel Marsh discovered a nearly complete skeleton of a huge dinosaur with only the skull missing. Marsh described the dinosaur, naming it *Brontosaurus*. However, two years earlier another man working for Marsh had found a large hip bone which Marsh named *Apatosaurus*. It was not until the 1960s that scientists realized that the hip bone was identical to that of the skeleton named *Brontosaurus*. Scientific procedure states that the first name applied to a genus must always be used in preference to later names. For this reason the animal known for generations as *Brontosaurus* was renamed *Apatosaurus*. Appropriately, *Apatosaurus* means 'deceptive reptile'. Similar confusions have arisen over other dinosaurs because of the fragmentary nature of fossil skeletons. The creature now known as *Apatosaurus* was a sauropod dinosaur. Like other sauropods, *Apatosaurus* was very large, measuring over 21m (70ft) in length and weighing around 30 tons, and had a small head perched on top of a long neck. It lived about 150 million years ago in North America. It was a close relative of *Diplodocus* (page 17).

Brachiosaurus

Brachiosaurus fossils have been found in North America and in North and East Africa and date back 140 million years. *Brachiosaurus* and several similar dinosaurs, such as *Ultrasaurus* (page 45), are highly unusual in that their front legs are longer than their rear limbs. In all other sauropod dinosaurs the rear legs are the longer. The reason for this curious feature is unknown, but it makes the brachiosaurids a highly distinctive group.

One adaptation to large size which is taken to extremes by *Brachiosaurus* is the presence of bone cavities known as pleurocels. The vertebrae of all sauropods are hollowed out so as to make them lighter, but without reducing their strength. The vertebrae of *Brachiosaurus* are so hollowed that in places the bone is as thin as paper.

By contrast the hip, shoulder and leg bones are extremely massive. These bones had to carry the enormous weight of the animal and so needed to be very strong. The legs were straight and pillar-like, ending in broad feet which would have been supported on a tough pad of skin and muscle. The front feet of *Brachiosaurus* were equipped with a single large claw. Nobody is quite certain what use this talon performed, but some scientists think it may have been a defensive weapon of some kind. A skeleton of *Brachiosaurus* in a museum in East Berlin is the largest dinosaur skeleton anywhere in the world. It is so large that a special hall needed to be built to house it.

Camptosaurus

Camptosaurus was the earliest of a long line of highly successful dinosaurs known as iguandontids. It lived 140 million years ago, before other types of iguanodontid appeared. The iguanodontids were perhaps the best adapted of all plant-eating dinosaurs, producing a wide variety of species and giving rise to other groups of dinosaurs. Several different species of *Camptosaurus* have been found worldwide, but they are all very similar animals and may be adaptations to local conditions.

Camptosaurus was a large plant-eating dinosaur which was 7m (23ft) long and may have weighed half a ton. It was capable of walking on its hind legs, as is shown by numerous fossilized footprints, but probably spent much of its time on all fours. The presence of a powerful wrist joint on the front feet indicates that they were used for walking. The mouth of *Camptosaurus* was well adapted for eating tough leaves and stems. The front of the mouth consisted of a tough beak which could crop vegetation. Further back the jaws were equipped with strong grinding teeth capable of pounding the leaves to an easily digestible mass. Scientists studying the jaws of the *Camptosaurus* believe that they have found evidence for the presence of muscular cheeks. These would have greatly aided the chewing process, enabling the animal to retain a mouthful of food for repeated mastication before swallowing.

Ceratosaurus

Ceratosaurus was one of the most unusual of the early hunting dinosaurs. In some ways it was very similar to *Allosaurus*, which lived at about the same time 150 million years ago, but in other respects it was very different. The basic skeleton of *Ceratosaurus* was similar to *Allosaurus*, with its two-legged stance and long tail, but was rather lighter. This may indicate that *Ceratosaurus* was able to move more quickly and was a more agile hunter than its larger cousin. The hip bones were fused together into a solid mass, which may suggest that they were subjected to the heavier stresses connected with running and leaping.

The most curious feature of this dinosaur, however, is to be found in the skull. *Ceratosaurus* sported a short bony horn in front of the eyes and over the snout. Only the bone core of this horn has been found, but some scientists believe that it may have been sheathed in a horny growth sprouting high above the skull. The purpose of this remarkable horn is unknown. It could hardly have been a defensive weapon, for *Ceratosaurus* was well equipped with dozens of sharp teeth and powerful talons with which to attack its prey. Some palaeontologists believe that the horn may have been used in fights between rival *Ceratosaurus* for possession of hunting territory or of a mate. Others believe that the 'horn' may not have been a weapon at all but simply used for display rather like a modern peacock's tail.

Coelophysis

This dinosaur lived about 210 million years ago, at the close of the Triassic period, and is the oldest dinosaur to be so completely known to modern science. In 1947 palaeontologists working at the Ghost Ranch in New Mexico came across an amazing deposit containing no less than a hundred *Coelophysis* skeletons. How so many animals of one species came to die together is not known, but it proved a great opportunity for the scientists. It was possible to study a large number of dinosaurs of the same species for the first time.

It was at once noticed that the creatures showed a wide diversity of size, the smallest individuals were just 1m (3ft) long while the largest were over 3m (10ft) long. All the skeletons of the animals were very similar however. The limb bones were thin and hollow, indicating an adaptation to lightness. Perhaps the *Coelophysis* relied upon speed and agility to catch its prey.

Such a supposition was borne out by the small, needle-sharp teeth of *Coelophysis* which indicated that the dinosaur fed upon small animals such as lizards and small mammals. The front legs too were consistent with this view for they were rather long and would have been able to grasp small prey animals. It is probably best to imagine herds of *Coelophysis* scampering through the Triassic landscape pouncing on smaller creatures and gulping them down.

Compsognathus

The honour of being the smallest adult dinosaur goes to *Compsognathus*. Smaller dinosaurs have been found, but these are the fossils of young, not of adults. The size of *Compsognathus* is truly extraordinary and contradicts the commonly held belief that dinosaurs were all large, clumsy animals. Adult *Compsognathus* were about the size and weight of a chicken, being about 60cm (2ft) in length.

Like chickens, the *Compsognathus* ran on its hind feet, and was most likely a very agile and swift runner. It was probably capable of running swiftly and executing dramatic changes of direction in order to catch equally fast lizards. One fossil skeleton of *Compsognathus* was found to contain tiny bones which seemed to come from a baby *Compsognathus*. This was originally taken as evidence that this dinosaur did not lay eggs but gave birth to live young. Other scientists suggested that the *Compsognathus* may have been guilty of cannibalism, but it is now generally accepted that the bones belonged to a lizard.

The first fossil of *Compsognathus* to be found was a complete skeleton which was excavated in Germany in 1861. The scientist who described this fossil was so struck by the delicacy and lightness of the skeleton that he gave it its name, which means 'pretty jaw'. This fossil dated back approximately 150 million years. Only one other fossil skeleton of this animal has been found (in southern France) so this dinosaur may have been rather rare.

Deinonychus

When, in 1969, the first full description of a *Deinonychus* fossil was produced it caused a great stir amongst palaeontologists. The dinosaur was so unlike previously known hunting dinosaurs that it was placed in an entirely new family, and upset several previously held convictions about carnivorous dinosaurs.

The head of *Deinonychus* is clearly well adapted to a lifestyle dependent upon hunting and killing other animals. The eyes were large and probably reasonably sharp. The jaws were worked by two pairs of muscles. One pair, the pterygoideus, could produce a fast, snapping action suited to inflicting fatal wounds on prey. The second, the capitimandibularis, were immensely strong and were able to bring the jaws together with great force. These latter muscles were probably used to tear chunks of meat from a victim once it had been killed.

However the most striking and unusual feature of the *Deinonychus* were its hind legs. These limbs were not only strong and powerful, but they were equipped with a frighteningly effective weapon. The second toe of each rear foot carried an enormous, sickle-shaped claw at least 12cm (5in) long. It was this which gave the animal its name, which means 'terrible claw'. The active *Deinonychus*, equipped with its claw would have been well able to attack and kill any other animal of its own size. The concept of the dinosaurs as slow, lumbering animals had to be discarded.

Diplodocus

One of the best known dinosaurs, and for many years the longest-known land animal, *Diplodocus* embodies many of the apparent inconsistencies of the largest dinosaurs. It lived 145 million years ago in North America. The animal was quite extraordinarily long, reaching over 28m (90ft) from snout to tail tip. Yet, at around 12 tons, it was lighter than many other dinosaurs reaching barely half this length. The comparatively light weight was due to the extremely slender neck and tail which accounted for most of the long measurement. Even the body was thin and slender compared to other sauropods.

The name of the *Diplodocus* means 'double beamed' and is sometimes taken to refer to the long neck and tail which project at either end of the body. In fact the name was given to the dinosaur because of a curious anatomical feature of the spinal cord.

The head of *Diplodocus* is especially confusing. It is almost absurdly small for such a large body. Clearly the skull contained a very small brain in proportion to body size, indicating that the animal may not have been particulary intelligent. More intriguing is the modest size of the mouth and the simple, peg-shape of the teeth. Whatever food the *Diplodocus* ate, and this is believed to have been vegetation, it cannot have required much chewing. The food must also have been highly nutritious to be adequate for such a large animal while only small amounts could be taken in by the tiny mouth. In fact, the problems of diet have not yet been solved and involve some highly complicated theories.

Dryosaurus

This dinosaur measured 4m (13ft) and was a member of the hypsilophodont family, which has been termed the 'gazelles of the dinosaur world'. In many ways hypsilophodonts, such as *Dryosaurus*, occupied a similar ecological role to the modern gazelles. They ate plants, as is shown by their teeth which are tough and heavily ridged to cope with the fibrous leaves and stems.

The front legs of *Dryosaurus* bore five fingers and were rather strong. It is probable that the hands gathered plant food and placed it in the mouth. In common with most other ornithischian dinosaurs, the front of the mouth of *Dryosaurus* lacked teeth, but carried a horny beak which was probably highly effective at cropping vegetation. *Dryosaurus* moved on its hind legs, and was clearly capable of great bursts of speed – the shins of *Dryosaurus* were much longer than the thighs (an adaptation to high speed running) and were powered by strong muscles.

It is probably best to imagine the *Dryosaurus* living in fairly open countryside such as plains dotted with scrub, and feeding on the low-lying vegetation. When danger threatened *Dryosaurus* would run off at high speed, relying on its fleetness to escape hunters.

Fossils of *Dryosaurus*, which date back 145 million years, have been found in both North America and Africa. At that time, these land masses were joined together and the Atlantic Ocean did not exist.

Edmontosaurus

Edmontosaurus was probably the largest of the hadrosaurs or duck-billed dinosaurs as they are sometimes known. Its total length may have been over 13m (42ft) and it reached well over 3 tons in weight. Like the rest of this family of dinosaurs, *Edmontosaurus* lived towards the end of the Age of Dinosaurs, this particular animal appearing about 68 million years ago.

As its name suggests, *Edmontosaurus* fossils were found near Edmonton in Canada, and it seems to have been restricted to western North America. A similar pattern of distribution has been found in other dinosaurs of the Late Cretaceous period. Scientists believe this to be evidence of a barrier between the western and eastern parts of North America. This may have been a shallow sea extending from the Gulf of Mexico to Hudson's Bay at this time.

Like other hadrosaurs, including *Hadrosaurus* (page 21) and *Saurolophus* (page 36), *Edmontosaurus* was adapted to a lifestyle which remains rather mysterious. These dinosaurs have webbed toes and a powerful tail which seems to be adapted to swimming. Some believe that the hadrosaurs led a largely aquatic lifestyle. However, the strong legs of *Edmontosaurus* show that it was quite capable of moving on dry land. Indeed, the small hooves on the front feet indicate that *Edmontosaurus* spent much of its time moving on all fours. Perhaps hadrosaurs spent time in the water when they were young and therefore vulnerable to attack by land-based carnivores.

Fabrosaurus

Fabrosaurus lived in South Africa about 210 million years ago and was one of the very earliest ornithischian dinosaurs. Some scientists have suggested that *Fabrosaurus*, or at least an animal very like it, was ancestral to all later bird-hipped dinosaurs. This conclusion is due to the fact that the body plan of *Fabrosaurus* is basically similar to that of later ornithischians and contains features consistent with it being an ancestral stock.

The body of *Fabrosaurus* was slender and light, and apparently adapted to rapid movement. The long tail was carried stiffly behind the animal when it ran, and served to counterbalance the body over the hips. *Fabrosaurus* would thus have been able to stand or walk on its hind legs while using its front legs for collecting food or other purposes. This small dinosaur, which was only about 90cm (3ft) in length, had neither armour nor weapons with which to protect itself from attack. *Fabrosaurus* probably ran away when threatened by a hunter. The teeth of *Fabrosaurus* were particularly distinctive. They were sharp, serrated and leaf-shaped. Such teeth were common in later ornithischian dinosaurs but were unknown in saurischians.

The first fossils of this dinosaur to be found consisted of only part of a jaw, found in 1964. Ten years later an almost complete skeleton was found, but some scientists do not think that it was identical with the jawbone found earlier. They prefer to give it a new name, *Lesothosaurus*, though the two would be very similar.

Hadrosaurus

This was the first animal whose fossils were found in America and recognized as belonging to a dinosaur. An almost complete skeleton was found in New Jersey in 1858, just 17 years after the British scholar Richard Owen first used the term 'dinosaur', to describe these early reptiles.

Hadrosaurus lived approximately 70 million years ago in North America and reached a length of 10m (32ft). The skull of *Hadrosaurus* shared many features with other members of the hadrosaurid family, such as *Edmontosaurus* (page 19) and *Parasaurolophus* (page 31).

The front of the mouth took the form of a broad, flat beak which lacked teeth but was covered by tough horn. Behind the beak was a large battery of extremely tough teeth. Several hundred individual teeth were contained in each jaw, and together they formed a highly efficient chewing mechanism. As the jaws moved up and down the angled teeth slipped past each other forming a grinding action. The rough surface of the teeth greatly increased their efficiency and enabled them to crush very tough plant food.

The actual diet of the hadrosaurs is still a mystery. The broad beak indicates that the dinosaurs scooped up their food, and implies a diet of aquatic plants. But the teeth prove that the animals ate tough food, such as pine needles. Scientists are not agreed over their diet, but the hadrosaurs were a very common group so whatever their food, there must have been plenty of it for them to eat.

Hylaeosaurus

Hylaeosaurus is a rather mysterious dinosaur. Only one fossil has ever been discovered, and that consists of only the front half of the animal. Another partial fossil found nearby consists of the rear half of an animal which has been named *Polacanthus*, but some scientists think that the two animals are really one and the same.

Such controversy apart, *Hylaeosaurus* is an important dinosaur, being a first in two ways. The fossil was found in a forest in Sussex in 1833, recognized as something unusual and sent to the British Museum. There it was given its name, which means 'forest reptile' and was studied by the great naturalist Sir Richard Owen. In 1851 Owen linked *Hylaeosaurus* with two other large prehistoric reptiles, *Iguanodon* (page 23) and *Megalosaurus* (page 26). He believed that they belonged to an extinct group of reptiles, which he named dinosaurs.

As well as being one of the first recognized dinosaurs, *Hylaeosaurus* was also the earliest of the armoured dinosaurs, living about 130 million years ago. The back of this 6m (20ft) animal was covered with thick bone plates which would have protected it from attack. Along its flanks and tail were large spikes of bone which would also have deterred any hunting dinosaur. Although slow-moving, *Hylaeosaurus* was probably fairly safe from attack.

Iguanodon

Iguanodon was a large herbivorous dinosaur, reaching 9.2m (30ft) and weighing around 5 tons. It lived about 120 million years ago in Europe. It probably walked on all four legs for much of the time, but was capable of moving on its hind limbs, perhaps when running. Like many later bipedal ornithischians, *Iguanodon* had large batteries of teeth which were highly efficient plant-crushers. The most remarkable feature of its front limbs were the hands which each bore not only weight-bearing hooves but also a large and extremely sharp thumb spike. The exact purpose of the thumb is unclear, but it might have been used as a defensive weapon of some kind.

Iguanodon was the second dinosaur ever to be named. Some fossil teeth of this dinosaur were found in 1825 in Sussex by a local man, Dr Gideon Mantell. Mantell noticed that the fossil teeth were the same shape as the teeth of modern iguana reptiles but were much larger. He named the prehistoric reptile *Iguanodon*, or 'iguana-tooth'. It was not until many years later that fossil bones were found which gave a clear picture of the appearance of *Iguanodon*.

The best collection of *Iguanodon* fossils came from 300m (1000ft) deep in a Belgian coal mine. The miners found the fossilized skeletons of 31 *Iguanodons* in a break in the coal deposits where an ancient ravine had once formed. It was thought that a herd of *Iguanodon* had tumbled into the ravine and died. The coal mine was closed down throughout the German occupation during the First World War and never reopened, so other fossils may still remain to be found.

Lambeosaurus

Like *Edmontosaurus* (page 19), *Lambeosaurus* belonged to the hadrosaurid or duck-billed group of dinosaurs which lived from about 90 million years ago onward. This means that it had a broad, flat beak at the front of its mouth and large teeth at the rear designed for crushing plant food. It was an extremely large animal, being about 15m (50ft) in length and having strong, heavy bones.

In common with some other hadrosaurids, *Lambeosaurus* sported a large bony crest on the top of its skull. The crest was hollow and consisted of thin bone through which ran the nasal passages. From the time of its earliest discovery, the crest of *Lambeosaurus* has been a subject of much controversy. Even today, scientists are not certain what function it performed. One of the earliest suggestions was that the crest acted as a snorkel while the dinosaur was submerged. This idea was based on the supposed aquatic lifestyle then thought to be common to all hadrosaurs. However, later researchers showed that the structure of the crest was very unsnorkel-like.

More recent suggestions have concentrated upon the air passages contained within the crest. The hollow crest may have acted as sounding box for the animal's cries, thus amplifying its voice. Alternatively, it may have contained very large scent organs, giving the animal a highly acute sense of smell. A third suggestion rests on the fact that the shape of the crests differed greatly between the various species of hadrosaur. Perhaps the crests were used as recognition signals at mating time.

Lexovisaurus

Lexovisaurus has the unique distinction of being named after a warlike tribe of ancient Celts. The Lexovi tribe once lived in the area of northern France where the fossils of this creature were later found.

Lexovisaurus belonged to the stegosaur group of herbivorous dinosaurs and shares many characteristics of that group. *Lexovisaurus* was a quadruped, but its hind legs were considerably longer than the front limbs, which might suggest that it was descended from a two-legged ancestor. The overall length of *Lexovisaurus* was about 5m (17ft) – rather smaller than other stegosaurs – and it had comparatively lightweight bones. The distinctive plates which ran along the backs of stegosaurs were more like spines in *Lexovisaurus*. The plates which jutted upward from the neck and back were thin and short, those along the tail were long and pointed. A pair of especially long spikes projected out from the hips. These spikes might have been for protection (although easily pushed aside) or for display.

Lexovisaurus lived about 160 million years ago, and seems to have been restricted to northern France and England. It is, therefore, the oldest known stegosaur and may be close to the animal which gave rise to all later members of this family, which was remarkably successful for about 20 million years and then faded away.

Megalosaurus

The first dinosaur fossils to be described belong to *Megalosaurus*, and were one of the three animals to which the term dinosaur was first given. *Megalosaurus* is typical of the large meat-eating dinosaurs which were common through the Jurassic and Cretaceous periods. Indeed, some scientists refer to these animals collectively as megalosaurs. Other scientists prefer to divide this group into a number of families.

The fossils of *Megalosaurus* were first discovered in 1824 and at once recognized as belonging to a large reptile. Early restorations showed *Megalosaurus* as a large, heavily built crocodile, but we now know that *Megalosaurus* walked on its hind legs, each of which had three toes armed with sharp talons. The front legs of the animal were much shorter but still powerful and were armed with three long claws. The hind legs may have been used to kill prey, while the hands would have been useful for tearing at meat and sinew. The skull of *Megalosaurus* was large and strong, and carried long jaws equipped with sharp curved teeth.

The animal was clearly a fearsome hunter and very able to deal with plant-eating dinosaurs of comparable size. Various species of *Megalosaurus* have been described which are mostly 9m (30ft) in length and weighing about a ton. They lived from 190 to 130 million years ago, although some experts believe this to be too long a period for one type of animal to have lived.

Monoclonius

Monoclonius lived about 80 million years ago in the western areas of North America. It was a 5.5m (18ft) plant-eater which belonged to the ceratopsid or horned dinosaur group. The body of *Monoclonius* was fairly typical of the ceratopsids. The four legs were strong and stout, supporting a heavy body and a short, dragging tail.

Monoclonius was powerfully built and was probably able to gallop at high speed for short distances. This could have been a defence mechanism, for the momentum built up by the animal would have made its horn a dangerous weapon to be used against predatory dinosaurs. It is the long horn which gives *Monoclonius* its name, meaning 'one horned'. The bone core of the weapon was probably sheathed with a horny substance, making it even longer than it would appear.

Behind the horn, the skull flared out into a wide frill. It has been suggested that this frill was a defensive guard to protect the animal's vulnerable neck from attack. However, in many types of ceratopsid (including *Monoclonius*) the bone structure of the frill had large openings in it which would have lightened it considerably but made it useless as armour. It is probable that the frill served instead as the base for strong jaw muscles which were used to power the teeth when grinding up tough plant food. The frill of *Monoclonius* is unique in that it has a pair of odd bony growths sprouting forwards over the frill. Some scientists prefer to call this animal *Centrosaurus*.

Nodosaurus

This dinosaur has given its name to a subdivision of the ankylosaurs: the armoured dinosaurs. Nodosaurs generally lived earlier than the true ankylosaurs and lacked the bony tail club and more sophisticated body armour of the latter. Different types of nodosaur have been found throughout North America, Europe and Asia, but not in Africa or South America. Fossils of a nodosaur were found in Australia in 1980, but only a foot and part of the back were unearthed so its appearance is uncertain. This distribution may show that the northern continents were separated from the southern hemisphere at the time the nodosaurs evolved.

Nodosaurus was a heavily built animal about 5.5m (18ft) in length, and lived about 95 million years ago in North America. Its legs were stout and muscular to support the great weight of the barrel-shaped body and its heavy armour. It is the armour which is the distinctive feature of *Nodosaurus*, being of an unusual pattern. The armour consisted of bands of large bone plates running from side to side, alternated with bands of small plates. Such an arrangement would have given solid protection from attack, but allowed the creature a great degree of flexibility. *Nodosaurus* probably lumbered through the vegetation, feeding on a variety of plantlife. When threatened it would have crouched down and relied on its armour to deter any predator. In most cases the armour would have protected *Nodosaurus*, but it would have been helpless if a predator could tip it on its back.

Ornithomimus

The name *Ornithomimus*, which means 'bird mimic', is highly appropriate for this dinosaur. Physically *Ornithomimus* was very like a modern ostrich, which has tempted many scientists to suppose that it had a similar lifestyle. The compact body of *Ornithomimus* was perched on top of long, muscular legs which were clearly adapted to high-speed running. Some studies suggest that *Ornithomimus* was capable of speeds approaching that of a galloping horse.

The small head was mounted on the end of a long, flexible neck, again like that of the ostrich. Unlike most other dinosaurs, *Ornithomimus* had no teeth whatsoever. Instead its delicate jaws were covered by a horny growth making them almost beak-like in structure. These similarities to the modern flightless bird might indicate that *Ornithomimus*, too, ran over open plains feeding on seeds, insects and plant food.

There are also differences from the ostrich. The most noticeable is that *Ornithomimus* had a long bony tail. However, this was probably simply used to balance the body when running and may not indicate a difference in lifestyle. More important were the arms and hands which were strong and equipped with long fingers. These indicate that although *Ornithomimus* may have inhabited plains and depended on speed for safety, it may not have fed as do ostriches.

This highly successful dinosaur lived in North America from 75 to 64 million years ago. It died out when all dinosaurs finally became extinct.

Ouranosaurus

Ouranosaurus was a large animal, about 7m (23ft) long, which was able to walk on either all fours or its hind legs only. It lived 120 million years ago, at the same time as *Iguanodon* (page 23), and inhabited northwest Africa. This dinosaur is grouped together with *Iguanodon*, but although it is basically similar, it has some unique and unusual features.

The skull is comparatively large and has two prominent bumps between the eyes and nostrils, the purpose of which is unknown. The jaws are very long, and end in a broad muzzle more like that of the hadrosaurs than that of an iguanodontid. However, the most noticeable difference between *Ouranosaurus* and other iguanodontids was the large upright frill which ran along its back. The frill was supported by long bony spines which grew upward from the vertebrae and were linked together by bony rods. This arrangement would have been inflexible and rigid. These bones were covered by skin to form a 'sail' which would have been fragile and vulnerable to attack from other dinosaurs.

The exact purpose of this remarkable sail is unknown, though several theories have been put forward. It has been suggested that the sail may have been used as a display in ritual contests between different *Ouranosaurus*. Alternatively the sail may have been used to soak up the warmth of the sun on chilly mornings.

Parasaurolophus

Parasaurolophus was one of the very last dinosaurs on Earth. It lived about 65 million years ago in western North America and seems to have become extinct at about the same time as dinosaurs were dying out throughout the world. Measuring 10m (33ft), *Parasaurolophus* had a comparatively heavily built skeleton for a hadrosaurid. The front legs were particularly robust, so this dinosaur may have spent more time walking on all fours than related dinosaurs such as *Lambeosaurus* (page 24) and *Edmontosaurus* (page 19).

The main difference between *Parasaurolophus* and other hadrosaurids is to be found in its skull. This creature carried a quite extraordinary crest of bone which swept back from the rear of its skull and was longer than the rest of the head. It has recently been suggested that a large flap of brightly coloured skin ran from the crest to the back of the neck, which would have been used as a signalling device in contests between rival *Parasaurolophus*, but there is as yet no evidence for this.

Until recently different species of *Parasaurolophus* were distinguished chiefly by the size and shape of the crest. Present opinion, however, holds that these different crest shapes do not represent species of dinosaur, but distinguish between sexes and ages within the same species. The short, curved crest of *Parasaurolophus cyrtocristatus*, for instance, has been re-interpreted as marking the female of the species.

Plateosaurus

Plateosaurus was the largest animal of its time, and represents an important stage in the development of the dinosaurs. Fossils of *Plateosaurus* has been found in large numbers in central Europe. Many complete skeletons have been found, often collected together in a single deposit. This curious concentration of good fossils has puzzled palaeontologists. It may be that *Plateosaurus* lived in an area which suffered periodic droughts. Especially severe droughts might have killed off *Plateosaurus* which had gathered at drying water holes. If this supposition were correct it would account for the unusual grouping of good fossils.

The overall length of *Plateosaurus* averaged 8m (26ft), most of which made up the long neck and tail. It probably spent most of its time walking on all fours, though it was able to rear on its hind legs. The front feet were equipped with hooked claws which may have been used for grasping vegetation.

Plateosaurus belonged to a group of dinosaurs known as prosauropods. These animals lived between 210 and 190 million years ago and were extremely common throughout the world. They seem to have been the first group of dinosaurs to adapt successfully to a vegetable diet. In the early Jurassic period the prosauropods were replaced by the giant sauropods such as *Brachiosaurus* (page 11) and *Diplodocus* (page 17). Some scientists believe that prosauropods were ancestral to sauropods, but others think the two groups simply evolved from a common ancestor.

Protoceratops

As its name might suggest *Protoceratops* was the earliest and most primitive of the ceratopsian, or horned, dinosaurs. It lived 85 million years ago. Later members of this group include *Monoclonius* (page 27) and *Triceratops* (page 43) and were much larger than *Protoceratops*.

Fossils of *Protoceratops* were first found by an American expedition which penetrated the wild and inaccessible Gobi Desert of Mongolia in 1922. The scientists found several complete skeletons of this dinosaur, and so were able to produce a fairly accurate picture of the animal. *Protoceratops* measured 2.8m (6ft) and weighed just over a ton. Though small, *Protoceratops* showed many features characteristic of later horned dinosaurs. It was a heavily built quadruped with powerful legs. The skull of this little dinosaur had a bony frill extending back over the neck which served as an anchoring point for powerful muscles which worked the strong jaws.

The scientists working in the Gobi were most excited by finds of nests belonging to *Protoceratops*. Before this date no dinosaur eggs had been found – now scientists had dozens of them. The eggs were arranged in circular nests and were laid in batches of about 14. Some fossils of baby *Protoceratops* were also found, showing these creatures to be about 28cm (1ft) in length. When these nests were found, it was thought that the adults laid their eggs and then abandoned them. However, in 1978 a hadrosaur nest was found with a group of partly grown young. This implies that the young stayed at the nest, and were probably cared for by their parents.

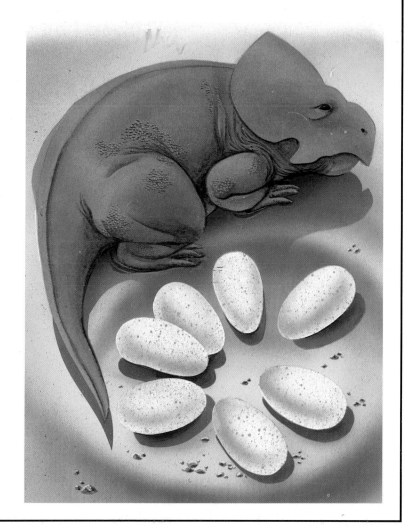

Psittacosaurus

Psittacosaurus lived about 95 million years ago in eastern Asia. Scientists studying this small dinosaur think that it may have been the ancestor of the later ceratopsian, or horned, dinosaurs such as *Protoceratops* (page 33) and *Triceratops* (page 43). This idea is based upon certain characteristics of the *Psittacosaurus* skeleton.

Like the later horned dinosaurs, *Psittacosaurus* has a pointed beak at the front of its mouth. This beak is toothless and covered by a tough horny growth. More importantly *Psittacosaurus* has a small bone, called the rostrum, in the upper jaw which is found only in ceratopsians. At the rear of the skull was a ridge of bone which may have served as a base for strong jaw muscles and could have then evolved into the elaborate frill of later horned dinosaurs. These two features are taken as signs that the *Psittacosaurus* later evolved into the horned dinosaurs.

However, if the *Psittacosaurus* did give rise to the ceratopsians, it had a long way to develop. *Psittacosaurus* was small, barely 90cm (3ft) in length and habitually moved on its hind legs. In fact the body of *Psittacosaurus* was very similar to those of a group of small herbivorous dinosaurs known as hypsilophodonts, which were related to the iguantodontids. Indeed, when the fossils were first discovered, it was thought that *Psittacosaurus* was merely another type of hypsilophodont. It is now fairly certain, however, that the horned dinosaurs evolved from the hypsilophodonts by way of *Psittacosaurus*.

Saltopus

The name of this small dinosaur means 'leaping foot' and was given to it because its discoverer thought that it might have jumped like a modern kangaroo. However, it is far more likely that this creature ran on its hind legs in a more normal manner. The fossil evidence for this creature consists of a single skeleton found in a quarry to the east of Inverness in 1910. The skeleton is incomplete, but there is enough to reveal the probable appearance and lifestyle of *Saltopus*.

Saltopus was just 60cm (2ft), and it probably weighed no more than a modern domestic cat. The comparatively long shins and toes of the animal suggest that it was able to run very quickly. Most of its limb bones were hollow, creating a strong, but light skeleton. These adaptations mean that

Saltopus was able to run very fast, and was extremely agile. It probably preyed upon small animals, such as lizards and insects, snapping them up in its small jaws.

Saltopus belonged to a group of dinosaurs known as coelophysids, including *Coelophysis* (page 14), which were fairly common towards the close of the Triassic period. Some scientists think that these animals may not have been closely related, but simply shared characteristics because they had a similar lifestyle. Whether or not they should be lumped together in a single group, the coelophysids were ancestral to many later types of small meat-eating dinosaur, such as *Compsognathus* (page 15).

Saurolophus

Like *Edmontosaurus* (page 19), and *Parasaurolophus* (page 31), *Saurolophus* was a hadrosaurid dinosaur living towards the end of the Age of the Dinosaurs and shared many characteristics. *Saurolophus* was about 9m (30ft) long and stood about 3m (10ft) tall at its hips. It may have walked on four legs for most of the time, but was able to run on its hind legs when it needed to do so. The forelimbs of this and other hadrosaurs were rather unusual. The 'fingers' were webbed, indicating that they were used for swimming, but the fingers also had hooves, which would have been used for walking. Perhaps these animals lived like the modern hippopotamus, and spent much of the day in water coming on to land at night.

The skull of *Saurolophus* is rather unusual in that it carries a small crest made of solid bone which projected backwards from the top of the skull. Most other hadrosaurids have either a hollow crest, or no crest at all. The small crest, and odd positioning of the nostrils, have caused some scientists to suggest that *Saurolophus* had a loose flap of skin over its forehead which could have been inflated and used to make a loud noise, rather like the croak of a modern frog.

Fossils of this large dinosaur have been found in both western North America and in eastern Asia, but nowhere else. Many other dinosaurs of this time show a similar distribution. Scientists believe that there was a land link across the Bering Straits along which dinosaurs could have travelled, but that shallow seas ran across both central North America and central Asia, thus creating a barrier to the movement of land dinosaurs.

Spinosaurus

Spinosaurus was an unusual meat-eating dinosaur which lived about 100 million years ago in northern Africa. The most striking feature of this dinosaur was the tall rigid sail of skin which ran along its back. This flap of skin was supported by tall blades of bone which rose up from its spine. The thin supporting bones would have made the sail rather fragile, and it might be thought that it would have been vulnerable when the *Spinosaurus* was attacking its prey animals. However, the tall sail must have had some advantage. It might have been used as a heat regulator, either absorbing heat from the sun or radiating heat to cool air. Others believe that the sail was used as a signalling device between *Spinosaurus*. Perhaps the animals signalled to each other to mark out territory or when trying to attract a mate.

Except for the sail, *Spinosaurus* was a fairly typical large meat-eating dinosaur. It measured 12m (40ft) in length, making it larger than most types, and was armed with sharp claws and teeth.

Spinosaurus was not the only meat-eater to sport a sail along its back. *Altispinax*, which lived in Britain about 125 million years ago, had a small sail over its shoulders, while *Metriacanthosaurus* had a short sail reaching from its neck to its tail. Some scientists think that these three dinosaurs should be grouped together as spinosaurids, but others believe that they were not related.

Staurikosaurus

Staurikosaurus is one of the earliest and most primitive dinosaurs known. It lived about 210 million years ago in South America, a partial fossil skeleton having been found a few miles north of the River Plate.

Staurikosaurus was a fairly small dinosaur being just over 2m (6ft) long. Much of this length was made up of a long, thin tail which served to balance the weight of the body so that the animal could move on its hind legs. The hind legs were clearly adapted to fast running but bore five toes, a primitive feature not found in later dinosaurs. The front legs were much shorter and were not used for walking. They also had five toes and may have been used in collecting food. The head was mounted on a short, flexible neck and was equipped with sharp teeth. It is probable that *Staurikosaurus* had a fairly mixed diet, including small animals as well as some vegetable matter.

The exact position of *Staurikosaurus* within the dinosaur evolutionary scene is unclear. It is a saurischian dinosaur, but its skeleton shows similarities with both the prosauropods, such as *Plateosaurus* (page 32) and with early meat-eaters such as *Coelophysis* (page 14). Perhaps *Staurikosaurus* was related to both groups, or it may have been on a line which died out without leaving any descendants.

Stegosaurus

Stegosaurus was both the largest and best known of the stegosaurs, or plated dinosaurs, to which it has given its name. It lived about 145 million years ago in North America and was nearly 9m (30ft) from head to tail.

The body of *Stegosaurus* was truly massive and probably weighed around 2 tons. It was supported on four pillar-like legs. The front limbs were much shorter than the hind legs, which might indicate that the animal was descended from bipedal ancestors. The skull of *Stegosaurus* was very small and contained jaws equipped with simple, leaf-shaped teeth. It is probable that *Stegosaurus* fed on low-lying plants and did not trouble to chew them before swallowing. Bacterial action in the stomach would have broken down the plant cells before digestion.

The most striking feature of *Stegosaurus* was the large plates which ran in a double row along its back. The largest of these bony plates was over 1m (3ft) tall, the smaller plates being found over the neck and tail. When fossils of *Stegosaurus* were first discovered in 1877 it was thought that the plates were a form of armour to protect the animal from attack. However, they are not firmly attached to the skeleton and could have been easily pushed aside. It is now thought that the plates may have been heat regulators. If the plates were covered with blood-rich skin the *Stegosaurus* needed only to stand in the sun to warm itself quickly, or to stand in the shade to cool down. Such an arrangement might have been of great use, because reptiles cannot sweat to lose heat.

Struthiomimus

Struthiomimus was one of the larger ostrich dinosaurs, or ornithomimids, which inhabited western North America and eastern Asia towards the close of the Age of the Dinosaurs about 70 million years ago. Relatively few fossils of *Struthiomimus* have been found, but those that are available for study can reveal much about the animal and its habits.

Like *Ornithomimus* (page 29), *Struthiomimus* strongly resembled a modern ostrich in general body plan. The long legs were clearly adapted to high-speed running over plains while the long neck was topped by a delicate head equipped with a long beak rather than tooth-filled jaws. The front limbs of *Struthiomimus* are particularly interesting. They are rather longer and stronger than in other ostrich dinosaurs, and were armed with three long curved claws. Scientists seeking to imagine a viable lifestyle for this unusual group of dinosaurs have made much of these arms. They seem to have been adapted for digging and grasping.

Many fossils of ostrich dinosaurs have been found in coastal and river deposits. It has, therefore, been suggested that these toothless dinosaurs preyed upon crabs, shrimps and other small aquatic animals. The long hands would have been used to scrape aside sand or mud and to reach between stones in the search for food. Not all scientists agree with this idea, preferring to picture *Struthiomimus* eating a mixed diet of fruit, leaves and insects.

Styracosaurus

Styracosaurus had perhaps the most unusual frill of any ceratopsian, or horned dinosaur. Unlike the frills of other ceratopsians, which were smooth or rather knobbly, that of *Styracosaurus* sported six long horns which reached backwards, curving over the back and flanks of the dinosaur. The function of these extraordinary horns is not immediately obvious. They are usually thought of as being defensive weapons for use against attacking carnivorous dinosaurs. However, these horns are not really orientated in a direction which would make them particularly effective.

The single upright nose horn would have been far more useful as a weapon. When threatened, the *Styracosaurus* could have charged forwards, using this horn in much the same way as a modern rhinoceros. It has been suggested that the growths sprouting from the frill were used in displays between *Styracosaurus* and rivals of the same species. It might have been shown in much the same way as modern male peacocks flaunt their tails. The frill would have lain flat along the neck and back, but when the animal wished to display, it would have bobbed its head, causing the frill to rise and fall in a dramatic fashion.

The body of *Styracosaurus* was fairly typical of ceratopsids. It measured about 5.5m (18ft) in length and was heavily built with a short tail. This animal is well known for a complete fossilized skeleton has been found, and is preserved in the American Museum of Natural History. It lived about 80 million years ago in the region that later became western Canada.

Thecodontosaurus

Thecodontosaurus was a prosauropod dinosaur, closely related to *Anchisaurus* (page 9), and shared many characteristics with other dinosaurs of this group. It had a long neck and tail at either end of a fairly heavy body. *Thecodontosaurus* was probably a plant-eater, though it might have preyed upon small animals as part of its diet. Reaching an overall length of just 2m (7ft) *Thecodontosaurus* was a small dinosaur which walked on all four legs, but could have reared up when feeding. It lived about 200 million years ago and was a widespread genus. Fossils of *Thecodontosaurus* have been found in both Britain and South Africa, and fragmentary fossils which may belong to this creature have also been unearthed in Australia.

The name *Thecodontosaurus* means 'reptile with teeth in sockets', and is a reference to this dinosaur's similarity to a group of reptiles known as the thecodonts. The thecodonts first evolved about 225 million years ago and are distinguished from other reptiles by having their teeth set in sockets in the jaw. All the thecodonts were four-legged meat-eaters which preyed on other reptiles. In time the thecodonts evolved into several other groups of reptiles which included the dinosaurs, the flying pterosaurs and the crocodiles. They were therefore an important group.

The similarity between *Thecodontosaurus* and its thecodont ancestors is taken as a primitive feature. *Thecodontosaurus* is probably very similar in appearance to the first dinosaurs of the Mesozoic Era.

Triceratops

This most famous horned dinosaurs came to light in 1889 when a cowboy found a fossilized skull weathering out of the soft rock in a gulch. The skull was sold to the collector Othniel Marsh who named and described *Triceratops* for the first time. Since then dozens of *Triceratops* fossils have been found, some of them nearly complete skeletons, which date to about 65 million years ago.

The overall length of this dinosaur was about 9m (30ft) and the weight around 7 tons, although individuals varied considerably. The well-preserved skulls of *Triceratops* have enabled scientists to distinguish 15 different species, though some believe some of the 'species' to be females or adolescents of the same species. There might have been far fewer types of *Triceratops* than is generally thought. The lifestyle of *Triceratops* can be reconstructed with some accuracy, although certain problems remain.

The large horns are generally thought to have been weapons for use against carnivorous dinosaurs. However, some scientists argue that the ceratopsians used their horns for fighting each other, rather as modern deer use their horns. Another source of controversy surrounds the food of ceratopsids. The teeth of these animals were sharp and designed more for slicing food than for grinding. Some experts think that this means these dinosaurs fed on juicy plants which required little chewing. Others believe that the ceratopsids ate a wide variety of plants, which were then kept in the stomach for long periods of time for digestion rather like modern cattle.

Tyrannosaurus

Largest and most powerful of the meat-eating dinosaurs, *Tyrannosaurus* existed about 65 million years ago and was one of the last dinosaurs on Earth. It lived in the same area and at the same time as *Triceratops* (page 43) and *Pachycephalosaurus* (page 4), on which it may have preyed. *Tyrannosaurus* was about 12m (40ft) long and could have weighed as much as 7 tons.

It walked on its hind legs, which were stout and muscular. The front legs were very small and had only two small claws. Their function is unclear, but they may possibly have been used by the *Tyrannosaurus* to brace itself when standing up. The head of this animal was large and powerful, measuring over 1.3m (4ft) in length. The jaws were filled with strong, curved teeth up to 18cm (7in). The teeth were not only sharp but were serrated like steak knives so as to be more efficient at cutting through meat.

Some scientists believe that *Tyrannosaurus* was an active hunter, stalking the large plant-eating dinosaurs which lived at the same time. They point to the large claws and teeth of *Tyrannosaurus* which would have made effective weapons. Most experts, however, believe that *Tyrannosaurus* could walk only very slowly and would have been unable to catch other dinosaurs. They think that this giant meat-eater may have been a scavenger, feeding on the bodies of dinosaurs which had already died. Perhaps, like modern lions, *Tyrannosaurus* found its food in both ways, scavenging where it could and preying upon slow dinosaurs that were injured, sick or old.

Ultrasaurus

This unusual dinosaur was found by James Jensen, an extrovert scientist who has been named 'Dinosaur Jim' by the press. Jensen found the fossils in 1979 in an area where he had earlier found other dinosaur fossils. The rocks where the fossils lay date back about 140 million years to the late Jurassic period.

The most amazing feature of the *Ultrasaurus* bones are their staggering size. A famous photograph published at the time of the excavations shows Jensen beside the shoulder blade, which is far taller than he is. The total size of *Ultrasaurus* has not yet been determined, but it would appear to have been over 31m (100ft) long. The weight of such a large animal would have been truly enormous, possibly as much as 120 tons, and is close to the size of the largest animal known today: the blue whale.

Ultrasaurus was very similar to *Brachiosaurus* (page 11), which lived at about the same time. The front legs of these sauropods were longer than the hind legs (an unusual feature in dinosaurs) and they had relatively short tails. It used to be thought that sauropods such as *Ultrasaurus* lived in water and ate aquatic plants. More recent suggestions are that they may have walked on dry land, browsing on the leaves of tall trees. Scientists are still undecided about the lifestyle of these giant animals.

Velociraptor

The name *Velociraptor* means 'swift plunderer' and is probably an accurate description of this animal's way of life. *Velociraptor* was a fairly small dinosaur, measuring 1.8m (6ft) in length. It ran on its hind legs – the front limbs being much shorter and bearing three very sharp claws which may have been used to grip prey. *Velociraptor* was a meat-eating dinosaur and actively hunted its prey. On each hind foot was a long, curved claw which would have been a very effective weapon. When attacking another dinosaur *Velociraptor* would have attempted to kick out with its strong back legs and so inflict a fatal wound. It is possible that *Velociraptor* hunted in packs so as to be able to tackle plant-eating dinosaurs larger than itself.

In 1971 a joint Polish–Mongolian expedition found a remarkable fossil of *Velociraptor* in the Gobi Desert. As the scientists uncovered the fossilized skeleton, they realized that a second dinosaur was gripped in the arms of the *Velociraptor*. This was found to be a *Protoceratops* (page 33). It seemed that the two dinosaurs had died together while the *Velociraptor* was trying to kill the *Protoceratops*. *Velociraptor* lived about 80 million years ago in eastern Asia, and was a relative of *Deinonychus* (page 16).